Philosophy 101

A Primer for the Apathetic or Struggling Student

Max Malikow

UNIVERSITY PRESS OF AMERICA,® INC.
Lanham • Boulder • New York • Toronto • Plymouth, UK

Copyright © 2009 by
University Press of America,® Inc.
4501 Forbes Boulevard
Suite 200
Lanham, Maryland 20706
UPA Acquisitions Department (301) 459-3366

Estover Road
Plymouth PL6 7PY
United Kingdom

All rights reserved
Printed in the United States of America
British Library Cataloging in Publication Information Available

Library of Congress Control Number: 2008943961
ISBN: 978-0-7618-4416-7 (paperback : alk. paper)
eISBN: 978-0-7618-4417-4

∞™ The paper used in this publication meets the minimum
requirements of American National Standard for Information
Sciences—Permanence of Paper for Printed Library Materials,
ANSI Z39.48—1984

Contents

Introduction		v
1	Epistemology	1
2	Logic	7
3	Ethics	13
4	Value Theory	17
5	Aesthetics	23
6	Metaphysics	27
Conclusion		35
Glossary		37
References		43

Introduction

I do not feel obliged to believe that the same God who has endowed us with sense, reason, and intellect has intended us to forego their use.

—Galileo Galilei

"Oh no, another philosophy book!" You would think that after twenty-six centuries of reflecting and writing, all that could be said about philosophy has been said. And since I admit that there is nothing new under the sun concerning the search for wisdom, it is reasonable to ask: "Why another philosophy book?"

This book is different not because of the information it provides but because of for whom it was written. In over twenty years of teaching philosophy I have encountered two types of students with whom I have sympathized—the apathetic student and the struggling student.

Perhaps you noted the word *primer* in the title. A primer is a textbook that explains the basic principles of a subject. If you are taking a philosophy course *only* because it is required of you, then this book was written for you—the apathetic student. Referring to you as apathetic is not intended as an insult. Apathetic simply means that the study of philosophy does not excite your interest. Apathy has no relationship with intelligence. You might be capable of understanding sophisticated philosophical material. This book will neither test your patience nor waste your time. It presents the fundamentals of philosophy in plain language with efficiency and a bit of humor.

The other student for whom this book was written is the student who is interested in philosophy but struggles to understand it. There are several ways in which a person can be intelligent. One psychologist, Howard Gardner, has presented a *theory of multiple intelligences* in which nine distinct types of intelligence are described. Two of these intelligences, *logical mathematical* and *existential*, are assets in the study of philosophy. Although you might be intelligent in a number of ways and perform with ease and excellence in several subjects, understanding philosophy is a struggle for you. This book was written for you. It is a kind of *Philosophy for Dummies* (again, no insult intended) in which complicated material is presented in simple language; using analogies, examples, and stories. (Actually, there is a book, *Philosophy for Dummies*, written by Tom Morris.)

Perhaps you have recognized that what you have been reading is written in the second person, the style used in informal communication. This style is used throughout this book. However, you should not infer from the informal tone that the subject has not been taken seriously. It has been said that effective teachers are effective simplifiers. Sophisticated ideas and profound truths are no less sophisticated or profound because the have been expressed in everyday language.

ABOUT THE SUBJECT

There is a saying, "Philosophy bakes no bread." It is easy to acquire the impression that philosophers are so heavenly minded that they are no earthly good. In fact, William James, a renown nineteenth philosopher, said:

... the philosophy which is so important in each of us not a technical matter; it is more or less a silent sense of what life honestly and deeply means.
... Philosophy is at once the most sublime and trivial of pursuits (1995, p. 1).

Similarly, Professor Timothy Luke Johnson has written:

Classical Greek philosophers Socrates, Plato, and Aristotle are fine—if thinking is what you want. But the word philosophy means "love of wisdom," not "love of thinking." What about solid advice about how to be a good father or friend; or how to grow old gracefully; or know what true happiness is? Where can you find philosophy that tells you not how to think well, but how to live well" (2007, p. 40)?

Over the years, from conversations I have had with students as well as reading their course evaluations, I have received three categories of criticism of philosophy: *relevance*, *understandability*, and *enjoyableness*.

The authors of one philosophy textbook admitted to the problem of relevancy with these words: "Philosophy is generally regarded as perhaps the most abstruse and abstract of all subjects, far removed from the affairs of ordinary life" (Popkin and Stroll, 1993, p. ix). In *What Does It Mean to Be Well Educated?* Alfie Kohn challenges teachers to nurture their students in *five habits of the mind* (2004, p.9). One of these habits is questioning the relevancy of what is being taught. A problem with philosophy that I have heard consistently expressed by students is their perception of the irrelevancy of the subject. One of these students referred to the title of a required textbook, *Questions that Matter*, and said, "If these are the questions that matter, I'd hate to see the ones that don't."

Many teachers, including philosophy professors, would do well to include a "So what?" component in their lectures. The "So what?" part of a lecture unambiguously states the application of the material to the lives of the students. If more professors answered the "So what?" question with clarity there might be fewer students like the one who wrote this poem.

> Irrelevant
> The alarm clock rings, I've overslept—
> it's eight o'clock . . . Oh damn!
> Descartes, help me with this one,
> say more than just, "I am."
>
> There's nothing in my closet that I want to wear.
> Immanuel Kant help a bit and doesn't really care.
>
> Now, what to eat for breakfast?
> Oh Sigmund, help my mood.
> I don't care about my past, the issue here is food.
>
> I check inside my pocket; I'm poor as poor can be.
> "Perspective!" Plato'd call it—he is no help to me.
>
> I consider all my issues, then ponder all of you:
> Your philosophic missions were not worth living through.
>
> Questions that I never asked and theories by the score;
> and then you wonder why I think philosophy's a bore.
> —Anonymous

Understandability is a problem in the study of philosophy because it includes so much that is abstract—concepts rather than material objects. For example, a courtroom is a material object and an individual on trial is a specific instance, but *justice* is a concept. The well-known Swiss psychologist Jean Piaget theorized four stages that human beings go through in the development of their mental ability. The fourth and most advanced stage, the *formal operational stage*, is characterized by the ability to think abstractly. As with any intellectual or physical activity, some people are better at abstract thinking than others. I recall how one of my students explained her struggle with philosophy: "Professor, I just don't think that way."

In addition to the criticisms of relevancy and understandability is philosophy's lack of enjoyableness. Of course, any subject that seems irrelevant and is difficult to grasp is not going to be enjoyable to study. As an illustration, consider this thought from the German philosopher Martin Heidegger: "(Existence) designates a mode of Being; specifically, the Being of those beings who stand open for the openness of Being in which they stand, standing it" (1956, p. 214).

Did you enjoy reading Heidegger's words? Did you find his thought easy to understand? Has your life been enriched by his analysis of "existence?" I am confident that you answered "no" to all three of these questions. How could anyone enjoy reading hundreds of pages and listening to hours of lectures consisting of expressions like Heidegger's?

A more subtle reason for not enjoying philosophy is that it often implies judgment of how we are conducting our lives. This is especially true of *ethical philosophy*—the study of right and wrong behavior. There is an adage that a preacher's sermon should comfort the afflicted and afflict the comfortable. A systematic study of how we *ought* to live might make us uncomfortable with some of our thoughts and behaviors. A feeling of guilt is never enjoyable.

These criticisms have substance and should be taken seriously. Taking them seriously means answering these questions: Is philosophy simple or complicated? If it is complicated, can it be taught with explanations that are comprehensible, but not simplistic? Is the study of philosophy merely an intellectual exercise or can it be applied to real-life situations? Why do some people so enjoy philosophy that they make a career of reading, writing, and teaching it? Is the enjoyment of philosophy a pleasure available to most people or an eccentric few?

IS PHILOSOPHY SIMPLE OR COMPLICATED?

Philosophy is both simple and complicated. Metaphorically, a child can wade in it and a genius can drown in it. It is similar to psychology in that it can be reduced to simple explanations or expounded upon in volumes. This section provides several simple explanations.

Philosophy and psychology are both concerned with human behavior. However, being different disciplines, they pursue answers to different questions. Psychology seeks to explain *why* people think, feel, and act as they do. Philosophy seeks to identify and justify how people *ought* to think, feel, and act.

A subcategory of psychology is psychotherapy, in which a mental health professional works with individuals to help them examine, understand, and possibly change certain of their thoughts, emotions, and behaviors. The brilliant psychiatrist Irvin Yalom wrote that psychotherapy engages the patient in answering two questions: (1) What do you really want? (2) Is your current lifestyle moving you closer to or farther from what you say you *really* want (1989, pp.3–4)? A third question would result from "farther from" being the answer to the second question. That would be, "Why are you pursuing a lifestyle that is contrary to what you want?" Long before Dr. Yalom provided this summary, Socrates said the same thing in a single sentence: "The unexamined life is not worth living" (Plato, *Apology,* 38A).

Predictably, psychology and philosophy converge on the question of the meaning of life. While this question has been subjected to centuries of philosophical speculation, three noteworthy psychiatrists have offered concise analyses. Sigmund Freud said that work and love constitute the meaning of life (1935, pp. 186–187). Carl Jung assessed man's search for meaning as a neurosis that only religion could cure (1933, p. 229). Holocaust survivor Viktor Frankl concluded that there is no single meaning to life. Rather, each of us is responsible for making meaningful the innumerable life situations in which we find ourselves (1959, pp.21–115).

Another common interest of philosophers and psychologists is *happiness*—considered by both as overall life contentment. Philosophers, from reflection, and psychologists, from research, have sought to enumerate the life conditions that contribute to happiness. William James considered it the ultimate motivation of human beings: "How to gain, how to keep, how to recover happiness is in fact for most men at all times the secret motive of all they do" (1994, p. 78). Aristotle characterized happiness as, "an activity of the soul, in accordance with perfect virtue" (*Nichomachean Ethics*, I.6). Psychologist David Myers' exhaustive investigation of the accomplished research on happiness yielded results that are remarkably similar to Aristotle's conclusion: Happy people are active in both work and recreation. Their lives include *flow* activities—things they enjoy doing. Also, they are living in a manner that is consistent with their moral code (1992, pp. 15–22, 205–207).

The aforementioned saying, "Philosophy bakes no bread," only appears to be true. Ideas have consequences—the principles we have embraced as truths influence our behavior. The mathematician and philosopher Bertrand Russell eloquently expressed that our lives are affected either by our own ideas or the ideas of others.

> The person who has no tincture of philosophy goes through life imprisoned in the prejudices derived from common sense, from the habitual beliefs of his age or his nation, and from the convictions which have grown up in his mind without the cooperation or consent of his deliberate reason (1910, p. 5).

A philosophy of life is unavoidable, even if it is recognized only in review. The Danish philosopher Soren Kierkegaard wrote, "Life can only be understood looking backward, but it must be lived forward" (Price, 2004, p.225). Some people recognize the principles that have guided their behavior by looking back on their decisions and actions. In other words, they deduce what they believe from what they have done. Other people are conscious of their principles and determine their actions from those principles.

Nevertheless, all of us live and learn. There is a reciprocating action between ideas and experiences that modify what we believe and how we behave. Sometimes, when new experiences contradict something we have believed, we will make an adjustment in that belief. For example, the Nobel laureate and Holocaust survivor Elie Wiesel had a pre-Holocaust belief in God. The experience of the concentration camps did not eradicate his belief in God's existence, but it did alter *what* he believed about God.

Other times, when an experience challenges something we have embraced as true, we reinterpret the experience to accommodate to our belief. Psychologists refer to such reinterpretation as *belief persistence* and it can reach the ludicrous proportions illustrated by the man who believed he was dead.

> A certain man believed himself to be dead, in spite of efforts by his friends and family to convince him otherwise. In exasperation, they insisted he meet with the family physician in the hope that the doctor would be able to change the man's mind. After examining the man and pointing out to him the various vital signs he showed, the man continued to insist that he was dead.
>
> The doctor then asked him, "Do dead men bleed?" The man paused a moment and answered, "No, dead men do not bleed." The doctor then made a slight incision in his patient's hand. When blood began to flow, the doctor then asked, "Well, what do you say now?" Stunned, the man then exclaimed, "Oh my, I was wrong. Dead men *do* bleed!"

RECAPITULATION: WHY I WROTE THIS BOOK

This book expresses my determination to help indifferent students enjoy the study of philosophy and appreciate what it has to offer in real-life situations. This book also was written for students who experience frustration in grasping philosophy in spite of their strenuous effort to understand it.

Professors Michael Bratman and John Perry have written:

> Human beings do things for reasons. We want certain things and we believe that acting in certain ways will get us those things. So we act. Rocks don't act for reasons, but we do. It's part of what makes us human. . . .
>
> Humans also reflect on and criticize the reasons we do things. Do we have good reasons for our reasons? Why do we want what we want? Why do we believe what we believe?
>
> Having the capacity to reflect on one's reasons is another part of being human. It's a capacity that divides us from most of our fellow animals. We not only believe things, we can think about why we believe things. We not only want things, we can ask ourselves why we want them (1999, p.1).

Psychology is not the only subject in which human beings are involved in studying themselves. I agree with Bratman and Perry that philosophy addresses our very humanness. Whether we engage in a formal study of philosophy or not, all of us practice philosophy. Each of the chapters of this book is concerned with a philosophical activity in which we often find ourselves occupied.

The first chapter presents epistemology, the theory of knowledge. This subcategory of philosophy addresses the question: *How can we be certain of anything we claim to know?*

The second chapter's topic is logic, the principles of reasoning. Logic pursues the question: *How can we be confident that a conclusion is the result of a reliable thought process?*

Chapter three addresses ethics, the study of moral right and wrong. The ethical question is: *Are there standards and procedures for determining ethical behavior?*

The subject of chapter four is value theory, arranging things in the order of their importance or worth. The challenge when determining relative value is: *What are the factors that make one thing more valuable than another?*

The fifth chapter, aesthetics, is related to value theory. Aesthetics refers to those things that are pleasing to the senses; beautiful to see or hear. The aesthetic questions are: *What makes someone or something aesthetically pleasing? How is beauty determined? What constitutes a work of art or a classic?*

Chapter six describes what is perhaps the most abstruse of philosophy's subcategories—metaphysics, the study of ultimate reality. In everyday life we interact with the physical world of objects and other people. The metaphysical question is: *Is there reality outside of the material world that cannot be perceived either by scientific investigation or the five senses?*

Chapter One

Epistemology

I am the wisest man alive, for I know one thing: and that is that I know nothing.

—Socrates

In 1981 there appeared a book with an odd title: *The Three Christs of Ypsilanti.* Its author, Dr. Milton Rokeach, was a psychologist on the staff of a psychiatric hospital in Ypsilanti, Michigan. There he discovered three patients deemed to be adrift from reality because each believed himself to be Jesus Christ. Dr. Rokeach conducted research that some might consider capricious when he arranged to have the three Christ claimants housed as roommates and placed together in group therapy. A psychologist's interest in the three Christs of Ypsilanti is not the same as that of a philosopher. A psychologist would be interested in the etiology (i.e. origin) of the psychotic delusion of these men. A philosopher would ask, "How can we be certain that at least one of these men is *not* Jesus Christ?" Logic, which is the topic of the next chapter, rules out the possibility that all three (or even two) of the men could be Jesus Christ.

Epistemology is defined as the theory of knowledge. To be engaged in the study of epistemology is to wrestle with this question: *When I claim to know something, how can I be certain that what I am claiming is actually true?* Merely believing something does not make it true. A man can be thoroughly convinced that he is Jesus Christ or Napoleon or Abraham Lincoln, but his belief, regardless of its intensity, does not establish it as a fact.

Why are some beliefs regarded with skepticism and others uncritically accepted as true? It is insufficient to say that whatever most people—say ninety-nine out of one-hundred—accept as true is actually true. (There was a time when ninety-nine out of one-hundred people believed that the earth was flat.)

The means for establishing truth depends on the nature of the belief. Some beliefs are investigated scientifically; others historically; and still others philosophically. Scientists, historians, and philosophers have different methods and standards for determining truth.

SCIENTIFIC TRUTH

It is likely that you were introduced to scientific truth in a science class back in elementary or middle school. The four step procedure known as the *scientific method* consists of *observation, hypothesis, experimentation,* and *conclusion. Observation* is simply a matter of paying attention to the experiences that arouse your curiosity. Curiosity, in turn, gives rise to the formulation of a *hypothesis*—a tentative explanation of a condition or an event. (A hypothesis is different from a theory. Both are tentative explanations, but unlike a theory, a hypothesis can be tested and either verified or falsified. A theory cannot be tested but has credibility because it is logical and consistent with established facts.) *Experimentation* is a laboratory investigation or other data gathering exercise that will empirically demonstrate the truthfulness or falsity of the hypothesis. The *conclusion* is the formal statement that the hypothesis has been proven or disproven.

HISTORICAL TRUTH

Although science is limited in its pursuit of knowledge, the pursuit of knowledge is not limited to science. Historical truth is knowledge of the past based on testimony. Witnesses to an event can provide spoken or written testimony. Testimony also can be provided by evidence. Historical truth might seem to you like a trial in a court of law because it is the kind of truth sought in criminal proceedings. Police officers investigating a crime; juries deliberating over guilt or non-guilt; as well as historians researching an event are all engaged in ascertaining truth from weighing testimony.

PHILOSOPHICAL TRUTH

There are some issues that cannot be addressed either by the scientific or historical method. For instance, the question, "Does God exist?" is neither a scientific nor an historical question. The existence of God is a metaphysical issue and, therefore, a philosophical question.

Philosophers utilize three tests in their pursuit of truth: *logic*, *pragmatism*, and *correspondence*. The statement, "There is no truth" is illogical because it is self-contradictory. If, in fact, there is no truth, this would apply to the statement itself. Ironically, the statement declares itself to be untrue.

Christian Science serves as an illustration of a belief system that fails to meet all three of the philosophical criteria for truth. Founded a few years after the Civil War by Mary Baker Eddy, the Church of Christ Scientist (official name) is a religion and system of healing that teaches disease, sin, and death are caused by errors in thinking and have no actual existence. In other words, disease, sin, and death are illusions—misperceptions of reality. How do Christian Science followers justify this belief? Their logic is that since God is the perfect and benevolent Creator, all that exists expresses God's perfection and benevolence. Since disease and death, as well as sinful behavior by human beings, would be imperfections; these imperfections actually do not exist.

Is this reasoning flawless or specious? An analysis of this doctrine of Christian Science shows it to be illogical. Regarding death, if death is an illusion would that not be evil? Christian Science simultaneously denies the existence of evil and affirms the existence of an evil illusion—death. This doctrine is self-contradictory and fails the philosopher's test of logic.

Further, is this teaching practical? Philosophers require of an idea that it be useful to people in the management of their lives. This is the test of pragmatism. Ideas have consequences and a 1986 manslaughter trial in Boston demonstrated that the consequences of some ideas can be tragic. David and Ginger Twitchell, parents of two-year-old Robyn Twitchell, relied on prayer rather than medical treatment for their son. After a five-day illness the child died from a treatable bowel obstruction. The *New York Times* reported the Twitchell trial as, "one of a growing number of cases involving children who have died under Christian Science care" (July 3, 1990). Sadly, David Twitchell testified at his trial, "If medicine would have saved (Robyn), I wish I had turned to it" (*New York Times*, July 3, 1990). While a spokesperson for the church stated that the issue in the Twitchell trial was the free exercise of religion, the state viewed Robyn Twitchell's death less idealistically. The parents were convicted of involuntary manslaughter and sentenced to ten years probation. (This verdict was overturned on appeal.)

The test of correspondence addresses the question: "Is this idea compatible with reality as demonstrated by science?" Concerning Christian Science followers, their belief about disease, sin, and death is inconsistent with what science has demonstrated about these conditions. Medical science treats diseases and pronounces death, showing that physicians consider neither disease nor death an illusion. Although I have no statistics to support my belief that most people view disease, sin, and death as actual phenomena, I am confident that a survey of a standard random sample would demonstrate that they do. Certainly, there would be many more Christian Science followers if the belief of illusion were widespread. Nevertheless, we must be mindful that truth is not established by what most people believe. The test of correspondence is an indicator of truth and, when combined with logic and pragmatism, helps philosophers weigh and consider truth claims.

TRUTH: ABSOLUTE OR RELATIVE?

The exclamation, "Absolutely!" is used to emphasize the certainty of something that is believed. When you say that you are *absolutely* certain about something, you are saying that there are no conditions that could make you change your mind. In contrast, if you are *relatively* certain about something, you are saying that there might be conditions that would change your mind. In fact, the term "relatively certain" is an oxymoron. Is truth absolute? Is truth relative? Is truth something that is sometimes absolute and other times relative, depending on what is being claimed? For a clearer understanding of the difference between absolute and relative truth, consider a decision made by the American Psychiatric Association approximately thirty years ago.

Homosexuality is a mental disease. Do you agree with this statement? Consider another statement on the same subject: *Until 1973 homosexuality was a mental disease, but this is no longer true.* Are you wondering, "How could something be a disease and then not be a disease?" This is the case with homosexuality as regarded by an organization of mental health professionals.

In 1973 a vote was taken by the American Psychiatric Association with the result that homosexuality was removed from the list of mental diseases. (This list was in the *Diagnostic and Statistical Manual* of the A.P.A.) The voting members, under pressure from gay activists, eliminated homosexuality as a mental illness on the ground that it was not treatable. Their rationale was that since no treatment existed for changing an individual's sexual orientation from homosexual to heterosexual then homosexuality could not be a mental illness. (Imagine the American Medical Association taking a vote and determining that a certain type of cancer is no longer a disease because it cannot be cured.)

If you believe that homosexuality *never* was a disease, even before 1973, then you hold this belief *absolutely*. In other words, under no conditions has homosexuality ever been a disease. If, however, you believe that homosexuality *was* an illness, but has not been a disease since 1973, then your thinking on this matter is *relative*. In other words, homosexuality is—or is not—a disease depending on the culture and time period.

In 1961 the notorious psychiatrist Thomas Szasz anticipated the controversy that led to the A.P.A.'s decision. In *The Myth of Mental Illness* he denounced the use of the term *mental illness*, arguing that the term is a misnomer. He repeated this view in a subsequent book:

> Disease means bodily disease. *Gould's Medical Dictionary* defines disease as a disturbance of the function or structure of an organ of the body. The mind (whatever it is) is not an organ of the body. Hence, it cannot be diseased in the same sense as the body can. . . . The concepts of mental health and mental illness are mythological concepts, used strategically to advance some social interests and retard others . . .(1973, p. 97).

A skeptic is a person who habitually doubts or questions conclusions that are accepted by most people. In fact, there was a school of Greek philosophers led by Pyrrho of Elis known as the *Skeptics*—derived from the Greek word "to examine." Yet, in a sense, every philosopher is a skeptic—calling into question things most people have uncritically accepted. The words of Socrates that introduced this chapter express the questioning spirit of the philosopher: "I am the wisest man alive, for I know one thing: and that is that I know nothing" (Price, 2004, p.18).

Chapter Two

Logic

The difference between genius and stupidity is that genius is limited.

—Albert Einstein

There are few books with a more appealing title than attorney Gerry Spence's *How to Argue and Win Every Time* (1996). One of the principles of effective argumentation is the *law of non-contradiction*. In a debate you know you have the advantage when you have caught your opponent in a contradiction. The well-known line from the movie *A Few Good Men*, "The truth? The truth? You can't handle the truth!" is preceded by Tom Cruise's character catching Jack Nicholson's character in a contradiction. Prince Hamlet implies his understanding of this law when he asks, "To be, or not to be?" (*Hamlet*, Act III, Scene 1). He recognizes the impossibility of simultaneously existing and not existing.

Logic is the subcategory of philosophy that is concerned with the principles of correct reasoning. Logical thinkers are those who can produce a sequence of thoughts in which each idea is built upon the previous idea. A widely circulated, unauthenticated response to a question asked on a chemistry test is a remarkable example of a logical progression. The question asked was: *Is Hell exothermic (gives off heat) or endothermic (absorbs heat)? Support your answer with a proof.* Most of the students wrote answers using Boyle's Law, which states that gas cools off when it expands and heats up when it is compressed. One student, however, wrote the following:

> First, we need to know how the mass of Hell is changing in time. So, we need to know the rate that souls are moving into Hell and the rate that they are leaving. I think we can safely assume that once a soul gets to Hell, it will not leave. Therefore, no souls are leaving. As for how many souls are entering Hell, let's

look at the different religions that exist in the world today. Some of these religions state that if you are not a member of their religion, you will go to Hell. Since there are more than one of these religions and since people do not belong to more than one religion, we can project that all people and all souls go to Hell. With birth and death rates as they are, we can expect the number of souls in hell to increase exponentially.

Now, we look at the rate of change of volume in Hell because Boyle's law states that in order for the temperature and pressure in Hell to remain the same, the volume of hell has to expand as souls are added. This gives two possibilities: (1) If Hell is expanding at a slower rate than the rate at which souls enter Hell, then the temperature and pressure in Hell will increase until all Hell breaks loose. (2) Of course, if Hell is expanding at a rate faster than the increase of souls in Hell, then the temperature and pressure will drop until Hell freezes over.

So, which is it? If we accept the postulate given me by Ms. Therese Banyan during my freshman year that, "It'll be a cold night in Hell before I sleep with you," and take into account the fact that I still have not succeeded in having sexual relations with her, then number two cannot be true. Thus, I am sure that Hell is exothermic. (Note: The student received an "A.")

In contrast, the following incredible, yet actual, exchange in a court case illustrates an attorney's failure to recognize the inconsistency between previous testimony and the lawyer's next question (Price, 2004, pp. 226–227).

Attorney: Doctor, how many autopsies have you performed on dead people?

Witness: All my autopsies are performed on dead people.

Attorney: Do you recall the time you examined the body?

Witness: The autopsy started around 8:30 p.m.

Attorney: And Mr. Dennington was dead at the time?

Witness: No, he was sitting on the table wondering why I was doing an autopsy.

Attorney: Doctor, before you performed the autopsy, did you check for a pulse?

Witness: No.

Attorney: Did you check for blood pressure?

Witness: No.

Attorney: Did you check for breathing?

Witness: No.

Attorney: So, then it is possible that the patient was alive when you began the autopsy?

Witness: No.

Attorney: How can you be so sure?

Witness: Because his brain was sitting on my desk in a jar.

Attorney: But could the patient have still been alive nevertheless?

Witness: It is possible that he could have been practicing law somewhere.

THE TOOLS OF LOGIC

A common instance of a principle of logic is the *syllogism*, a form of reasoning consisting of a general statement (major premise), specific statement (minor premise), and conclusion. The oft used illustration of a syllogism found in many textbooks is:

All men are mortal.
Socrates is a man.
Therefore, Socrates is mortal.

A syllogism is a type of deductive reasoning—reasoning from a general statement ("All men are mortal") to a specific statement ("Socrates is mortal"). Another example of deductive reasoning is one you might have encountered in geometry:

A is equal to B.
B is equal to C.
Therefore, A is equal to C.

It is logical (i.e. correct reasoning) that two things (A and C) that are equal to the same thing (B) are equal to each other. The correctness of this reasoning can be *empirically* demonstrated. Empirical demonstrations establish something as true by way of experimenting rather than theorizing. Imagine taking three equal weights; labeling them A, B, and C; and placing them on a balancing scale in the following order:

Trial One: A and B
Trial Two: B and C
Trial Three: A and C

If all three trials result in the weights showing balance then the deductive reasoning would be demonstrated as correct.

It is not always possible to substantiate ideas by empirical demonstration. Such demonstrations result from the application of the scientific method and, as previously stated, science is limited in its pursuit of knowledge. However, as also previously stated, the pursuit of knowledge is not limited to science. In their quest for truth, philosophers carefully examine arguments. The word *argument* is derived from the Latin *argumentum*. While an argument can mean an angry dispute, in philosophy an argument is understood as the reason or reasons for believing something. When lawyers present a case in a court of law they are said to be making an argument. (By the way, it is not unusual for lawyers to have performed well in their philosophy classes, since both law and philosophy require argumentation.)

A *fallacy* is a mistake in reasoning that results in a flawed argument. Some fallacies are produced by illogical reasoning. For example:

All U.S. Presidents have been males.
Abraham Lincoln was a male.
Therefore, Abraham Lincoln was a U.S. President.

It is true that as of 2008 all U.S. Presidents have been male. It is also true that Abraham Lincoln was both male and a U.S. President. The fallacy in this reasoning is the inclusion of the word *therefore* in the syllogism. It does not follow that Lincoln was a U.S. president from the two statements that preceded the conclusion. The error in this syllogism can be shown more clearly by replacing "Abraham Lincoln" with "William Shakespeare."

Fallacies can also result from giving reasons that are irrelevant. An example of the fallacy known as *argumentum ad hominem* ("appeal to man") is the following statement: "Professor Smith's view on abortion cannot be taken seriously because he is a born-again Christian." In this example the merits of Professor Smith's position on abortion are not given consideration because of who he is. An argument cannot be refuted by degrading, trivializing, or in some other way pointing to the person who has presented the argument. Another instance of *argumentum ad hominem* is the advice to "consider the source" when receiving a criticism. To immediately dismiss a criticism *because* of the source is unwise. If a student complains that a professor has bad breath and the professor disregards the complaint because it came from a "D" student, it does not establish that the professor's breath is not offensive. We might not think highly of a person who criticizes us. Nevertheless, the criticism might be valid. Instead of "considering the source," consider the saying, "Even a blind squirrel finds a nut."

A saying with which you are likely familiar is, "Might makes right." The fact is, might does not make right. The fallacy illustrated by, "Might makes right" is *argumentum ad baculum* ("appeal to force"). It would be absurd to believe that intimidation or pressure of any kind establishes something as true. Imagine a gun placed to your head and under the threat of death you declared, "One plus one equals three." That would not establish three as the correct sum, not even in your mind. Fear might influence people to say something; but it can never force them to believe anything. Hence the proverb: *A man convinced against his will is a man unconvinced still.*

Argumentum ad ignorantiam ("appeal to ignorance") affirms the truth of something on the basis of a lack of evidence to the contrary. In debates concerning the existence of God it is not uncommon to hear the Russian cosmonaut Yuri Gagarin quoted: "I have been to outer space and I did not see God out there." Gagarin's statement makes no contribution to the discussion of God's existence. Absence of proof is not proof of absence. In this case, the absence of proof of the existence of God does not prove that God does not exist. If we heard a person say, "I looked everywhere and couldn't find my car keys," we would not conclude that the keys do not exist. We would conclude that they exist outside of the range of the search. Ironic is that there is no evidence that Gagarin ever said what has been attributed to him. Anyone who would use the quotation to refute the existence of God would have to concede that the cosmonaut never spoke it. Why? Because there is an absence of proof that Gagarin ever made the statement.

Argumentum ad vercundiam ("appeal to authority") is often used in advertising. In this fallacy an unqualified person provides testimony that is meaningless unless given by an expert. This is not a contradiction of what was said previously about "considering the source." In *argumentum ad vercundiam* the individual's education and experience are irrelevant to the opinion given. It is one thing for a famous athlete to endorse a breakfast cereal by saying, "I love the taste." It is another thing for that athlete to say, "This is the cereal for anyone who is concerned about LDL cholesterol and trans-fatty acids." In legal proceedings, expert witnesses are asked about their credentials in order to establish themselves as experts before offering an opinion.

Fallacies of *causal connection* occur when there is a misunderstanding between *cause* and *effect*. An example of this fallacy is a borrowed car with a flat tire. If the owner of the car said to the borrower, "I drive that car every day and never get a flat tire; you drive it once and get a flat," the implication is that the flat tire is the borrower's fault. In this case, the owner-accuser is disregarding the principle: *Event-A preceding event B is insufficient to prove that A is the cause of B*. Another illustration of this principle is the driver in a hurry who gets a red light and complains, "Every time I'm in a hurry I get *this* red light." The implication in this statement is that event-A (being in a hurry) not only occurred before event-B (getting the red light) but being in a hurry is the *cause* of getting the red light.

Another common misunderstanding of cause-and-effect relationships is their confusion with *correlations*. In a cause-and-effect relationship, event-A not only precedes event-B, but it can be demonstrated that A is the cause of B. A correlation exists when two events *tend* to occur together, calling for further investigation. For example, a study conducted by the eminent psychologist Edwin Shneidman showed a high occurrence of suicide among geniuses. The rate of suicide among the general population of the United States is one per sixty-thousand. The rate of suicide among the individuals in Shneidman's study with an I.Q. greater than 140 is one per fifty-five (Shneidman, 1996, pp. 84–86). This finding suggests a correlation between genius and the accomplishment of suicide. If being a genius and committing suicide had a cause-and-effect relationship then all geniuses would commit suicide.

Incorrect conclusions can sometimes be attributed to *overgeneralization*. This has occurred when too much is said from too little data. Early in my teaching career I served as a middle-school Social Studies teacher. When going over a test it was not unusual for one of my students to try to make the case that a question was too difficult by saying, "Everybody missed that question." I would then respond by asking, "Did you ask everybody in the class about this question?" Of course, the protestor had asked only one or two nearby students who also happen to have missed the question. From the item analysis of the test results, I already knew that only a few in the class had missed the question. This is a case of a student saying too much from too little data. It is understandable that people often believe that their experience is the same as nearly everybody else's. However, a single case, referred to as *anecdotal data*, is insufficient to represent a group.

A simple explanation is always preferable to one that is complicated. However, often a simple explanation is not correct. A *plausible rival hypothesis* is an alternative explanation that is just as believable as one that has been tentatively accepted. One explanation for a crowded restaurant might be that it is an excellent place to dine. However, a plausible rival hypothesis might be that it is Sunday and the restaurant is the only one in the city open on Sundays.

Similar to a plausible rival hypothesis is an *intervening variable*. An intervening variable is a condition that co-exists with another condition and might explain an event. For example, the suicide of a psychiatrist or police officer might be explained by the nature of their work. Both are intimately involved in the sadness and tragedies of human beings. The suicide of a psychiatrist or police officer could be attributed to their daily exposure to the pain of others. However, one factor that contributes to accomplished suicides is the availability of the means for killing one's self. Police officers have guns and psychiatrists are medical doctors with immediate access to lethal medications and the knowledge of how to use them fatally.

Chapter Three

Ethics

Anyone, then, who knows the good he ought to do and doesn't do it, sins.

—James 4:17

Assume a virtue if you have it not.

—Hamlet, Act III, Scene 4

Winchester, Massachusetts is a quaint little town located seven miles north of Boston. Its numerous colonial homes fronted by impeccably manicured lawns and charming town center contribute to Winchester being one of New England's priciest communities. Not that any town would have disregarded the invasion, but the pristine state of Winchester prior to the arrival of the geese made their intrusion especially troubling.

These were Canadian geese, a breed so large that they walked about fearlessly with an air of entitlement. A child licking an ice cream cone or snacking on a cookie in proximity to the geese did so at risk. Hundreds of these geese deployed as dozens of flocks deposited their cigar-sized droppings all over town, as if to mark their territory. When the undeniable became intolerable, a town meeting was called to address the problem. Subsequent meetings became necessary as each attempt to relocate the unwanted birds failed.

Eventually, there came the meeting at which killing the geese was discussed. Those who advocated termination suggested paying hunters a bounty for each goose carcass. Some at the meeting rejected this strategy, citing an understandable safety concern. Still others at the meeting made an impassioned moral plea against killing the intruders on the ground that the birds had a right to live, however bothersome and repugnant they might be.

The next chapter addresses *value theory*—the subcategory of philosophy that pursues an answer to the question: *What are the factors that make one thing worth more than another?* Clearly, the Winchester situation was an instance of competing interests with the best interests of the residents in conflict with those of the geese. How could the cleanliness and pleasantness of the town be weighed against the lives of the geese? When there is no scale for balancing the competing rights of parties, then the matter in question must be resolved by the application of principles.

Ethical philosophy is concerned with right conduct. The questions addressed in ethical philosophy are: *What makes some behaviors right and others wrong? What is the standard or code of conduct that determines right behavior?* In a Hindu culture the invasion of the Canadian geese would not be a problem. The Hindu doctrine of *ahimsa* teaches nonviolence to all living things. This principle is found in the sacred Hindu writings, the *Vedas*, which provide the code of conduct for Hindus. Of course, non-Hindus are not obligated to follow vedic teaching.

The necessity of a standard for determining ethical behavior can be seen by considering two events from World War II. The Holocaust was a government program of Nazi-era Germany by which six-million Jewish people were intentionally put to death. This genocide occurred not because of anything these people had done, but because of who they were—Jews! At the postwar Nuremburg trials the Nazis believed to have been responsible for the Holocaust were charged with "crimes against humanity." Most of the accused offered the defense: "I was merely following orders." Certainly, there is some merit in this justification. Tennyson's classic poem, "The Charge of the Light Brigade," is a tribute to soldiers who do their duty without questioning an order: "Their's not to reason why; their's but to do and die" (1870). Yet, is such obedience always morally right? Are soldiers acting ethically when they obey an order that goes against their conscience or sense of human decency? The Nuremburg tribunal could not have made a judgment without a standard for determining ethical behavior.

The Second World War also included the atomic bombings of Hiroshima and Nagasaki. Over 100,000 Japanese were killed in this action, most of them civilians. What is the moral standard for evaluating this decision by President Harry Truman? Is the maxim, "All is fair in love and war" an adequate justification? The Premier of Japan during the war, Hideki Tojo, was hanged as a war criminal three years after the war. If the United States had lost the war, would this have been President Truman's fate?

The moral questions generated by the Holocaust and atomic bombings require a standard against which to measure these events. In *An Essay on Man*, Alexander Pope wrote, "Whatever is, is right" (circa 1744). With all due respect to Pope, a brilliant man, if "Whatever is, is right," then there would be no ethical discussions. If you agree with Pope's statement and consider ethical philosophy unnecessary, perhaps you will reconsider your position after reading the following parable.

> Once upon a time there was a man sent by his king to recruit archers for the king's army. The man searched far and wide but could not find even one man skilled with bow-and-arrow to serve the king. Finally, coming upon a small village, he delighted in taking note of targets painted on the sides of numerous buildings, trees, and hillsides. He was delighted because each of the targets had an arrow in the dead center, "bull's eye" location. Excitedly, he asked the first man he saw, "Who is the master archer who lives in this village? He is needed for the king's army."
> The man of the village responded with, "We have no such man in this village!"
> The king's agent then asked, "But what about all these targets with arrows in the dead center?"
> The villager replied with a laugh, "Oh, those things! Those are from Shlomo, our village idiot. He goes around shooting arrows all over the place and when he finds one he paints a target around it.

Since Shlomo's target is determined by wherever his arrow lands, his bull's eye is a meaningless accomplishment. In ethics, if there is no pre-existing standard for a behavior, there can be no meaningful evaluation of that behavior as right or wrong. In ethical philosophy there are two types of targets: *teleological* and *deontological*.

A TELEOLOGICAL APPROACH TO ETHICS

In philosophy, it is often the case that a philosophical term is derived from a Greek word. The Greek word *telos* means "end." If we think of an *end* as a *goal*, then the meaning of teleological is easy to understand. To evaluate an action teleologically is to consider it according to a goal. Perhaps you have heard the saying: "The end justifies the means." In a teleological approach to ethics, behaviors are determined as right or wrong according to a desired goal. For example, in the Woody Allen movie, "Crimes and Misdemeanors," a prominent doctor has decided to end his two-year affair with his emotionally unstable mistress. When he informed her of his decision, she threatened to ruin his marriage by telling his wife. When he was unsuccessful in reasoning with her, he took his brother's advice and arranged to have the mistress killed. Teleologically, since the doctor's goal was to silence the mistress and save his marriage, the killing of the mistress was right.

A DEONTOLOGICAL APPROACH TO ETHICS

If you believe that the killing of the mistress was *wrong*, it suggests that you have evaluated the doctor's behavior deontologically. Deontological is derived from the Greek word *deon*, which means "duty." In a deontological approach to ethics, behaviors are evaluated according to pre-existing principles that we have a duty to obey. The doctor's action was wrong if measured against the biblical commandment, "Thou shalt not kill," or the principle of the golden rule, "Do unto others as you would have them do unto you." A third principle that could be applied is, "Two wrongs do not make a right."

CONCLUSION

The citizens of Winchester who argued for killing the geese took a teleological approach to the problem. Those who opposed killing the geese did so on deontological grounds. President Truman teleologically defended his decision to order the atomic bombings of Hiroshima and Nagasaki. His goal was to end the war with a minimal loss of American lives. Those who believe Truman acted unethically have argued that he violated the principle of war that forbids the intentional killing of civilians.

The parable of Shlomo demonstrates the foolishness of conforming the standard of excellence to the previously accomplished behavior. The Nuremburg trials raised the question of opposing obligations. *What are soldiers to do when duty conflicts with conscience?*

There is a relationship between ethical decision-making and happiness. Psychiatrist Thomas Szasz wrote: "The quality of our life depends largely on concordance or discordance between our desires and our duties. If we can define and experience our duty as desire—then we are happy, well-adjusted, normal" (1973, p. 47). As previously stated, Aristotle taught that we cannot be happy living contrary to our moral code (*Nichomachean Ethics*, I.6.).

Plato described the dynamic that occurs in us when we experience a conflict between duty and desire. His concept of the mind was that it consisted of three parts: *reason*, *appetites*, and *spirited element* (Martin, 1995, pp. 45-47). Reason informs us as to the right course of action—our duty. Appetites influence us in the direction of that which feels good—desire. The spirited element can be understood as the answer to this question: *What kind of person do I want to be?* Of course, life moves along pleasantly when what we *feel* like doing is what we *ought* to do. However, when duty and desire are in conflict, if the spirited element is strong enough, it will supplement reason and we will do our duty.

Chapter Four

Value Theory

What good is it for a man to gain the whole world, yet forfeit his soul?
—Jesus Christ (Mark 8:36)

A horse, a horse, my kingdom for a horse.
—*King Richard*, Act V, Scene 4

What would a man value so much that he would literally give his right arm to have it? If the man is Aron Ralston, the answer is *his life*. Trapped in a Utah cave when an 800-pound boulder shifted and pinned his arm against the cave's wall, after five days of futility he decided to do the only thing that would save his life. Neither his self-surgery nor his description of it was delicate. At a press conference he described the three-step procedure of cutting (flesh, muscle, and tendons), breaking (ulna and radius bones), and snipping (nerve). Despite being weakened by a forty-five pound weight loss, Aron Ralston accomplished the amputation that saved his life.

Value theory is the subcategory of philosophy that addresses the relative worth of things. It pursues answers to questions like, "How do people decide what to take with them when they have to leave their homes because of fire or flood?" and "Why is it cost-effective for the New York Yankees to pay Alex Rodriguez twenty-five million dollars a year?" The worth of something is always assessed in a context. Under normal conditions; air, water, and a match are of no great value. But to a drowning man; a man on fire; and a man freezing in the wilderness; air, water, and a match, respectively, are priceless. Aron Ralston's arm is something he never considered sacrificing until he had to choose between it and his life. Interesting and ironic is that a frequently used hyperbolic statement is, "I would give my right arm for x." Other familiar declarations that imply value are, "I would not trade x for anything," and, "Your money or your life?"

In 1972 an airplane carrying a Uruguayan rugby team crashed in the Andes between Argentina and Chile. Several of the survivors resorted to cannibalism, eating flesh from the frozen bodies of those killed in the crash. Like Aron Ralston, they did the unthinkable in order to survive.

It is one thing to believe that no one's life is more valuable than someone else's. Yet, there have been extraordinary situations in which the lives of human beings have been prioritized. The classic example of this is the *dilemma of the lifeboat*, in which decisions had to be made about who would remain in the boat and who would be set adrift, lest the overcrowded vessel sink. In this circumstance, a strong, uninjured man able to row had more value than an elderly, severely wounded survivor.

TEN ORDINARY INSTANCES OF VALUE THEORY

Given the rarity of self-amputations, decisions about cannibalism, and lifeboat dilemmas, it is understandable to ask: *What is the place of value theory in ordinary life?* Actually, decisions of relative worth are so common that they often go unrecognized as instances of value theory. Consider the following examples and do not be surprised if several of them describe decisions you have made. (Note that these examples call for decisions that are neither *right* nor *wrong*. These are decisions to be made by establishing a priority rather than conforming to a principle.)

1. You have promised yourself not to withdraw money from your savings account, but the lap-top computer you have wanted is on sale. Which is more important to you: a continually growing savings account or the computer?
2. You recently recounted to a friend the joys and benefits of being single. Soon afterward you meet someone and find yourself considering marriage. Which do you value more: freedom without commitment or lifetime companionship with someone you love?
3. You have a job that you consider mediocre; but your employer is financially stable and pays you adequately. Nevertheless, you keep thinking about starting your own business, working for yourself at something you love. Which will you choose: security or excitement?
4. You have been diagnosed with cancer. Your oncologist has told you that the chemotherapy that might save your life will be painful and make you so ill that it will render you bedridden. Your doctor has also told you that

without the chemotherapy you will feel healthy and normal for approximately six months and then rapidly decline in health and die within a year. Which would mean more to you: the possibility of being cured or six months of feeling healthy and being active?
5. After promising your best friend confidentiality, he confesses that he is sexually attracted to children, although he has never acted on this preference. Since he is an elementary school teacher, you urge him to resign his position. He refuses, claiming that he would never risk his career by being sexually involved with a child. You consider informing the principal of the school where your friend teaches what you know. Which is more important to you: your friend's career and his friendship or the precaution against a child being harmed and your friend going to prison?
6. You are stopped by a police officer at 11:00 p.m. on a Saturday. When you are asked, "How many drinks have you had?" you are afraid to tell the truth because you have had three glasses of wine in the previous two hours. Although the thought of lying is repugnant to you, you do not believe that you are driving impaired and you are afraid that the truth will not serve you well. Which do you value more: truthfulness or expediency?
7. Your dream is to work as a professional actor. After starring in high school and college plays, you have had little success in New York and California. After several years of nothing more than work in television commercials and as an extra, you are offered a high school position teaching English and drama. Which will you choose: persisting at fulfilling a dream or abandoning your dream to begin a teaching career in your hometown?
8. You have saved $5,000 for the purchase of a used car to replace the car you have been driving. While looking for a car you are attracted to a new car that would cost $20,000. Although you hate the idea of car payments for the next five years, you consider making a $5,000 down payment and paying $375 per month for the next sixty months. Which will you choose: a new car with payments or a used car without them?
9. You have the opportunity to move into a one-bedroom apartment with a monthly rent of $600. The thought of living alone appeals to you. A friend is also looking for a place to live and asks you if you would like to share a two-bedroom apartment for one-half of the rent. This would cost you $400 per month. The apartments are comparable. It is your preference to live alone, but the opportunity to save $200 per month is attractive. Which do you value more: privacy or saving money?
10. You are strongly attracted to someone you recently met at school. Fearing rejection, you have not made an attempt to get together outside of class. Soon the semester will be over and the opportunity to pursue a

relationship will be lost—perhaps permanently. If you do not risk the pain of rejection you will be left to wonder what would have happened if you had tried. Which do you value more: safety or resolution?

CASE STUDY: PROFIT OR PRODUCT SAFETY?

Psychiatrist Scott Peck has written: "Triggers are pulled by individuals. Orders are given and executed by individuals. In the last analysis, every single human act is ultimately the result of an individual choice" (1985, p. 215). Product liability lawsuits occur when there is a claim that a manufacturer is responsible for injury or damage caused by a product. Of course, it would be ridiculous to hold the manufacturer of a hunting rifle responsible for a murder if the rifle was used in a homicide. However, if the rifle backfired and killed the hunter using it, then it is likely that the manufacturer would face a product liability lawsuit.

Perhaps the most famous of these cases is the one that involved the Ford Pinto, an American subcompact car introduced by the Ford Motor Company in 1971 and produced until 1980. When it appeared in 1971, Pinto sales were so brisk that the plain, but fuel-efficient subcompact car was dubbed, "the car nobody loves, but everybody buys." Before its ten-year production run was over it became "the barbeque that seats four." What happened to this affordable little car that reduced it from popularity to a punchline? (In the movie "Speed" Sandra Bullock's character, Annie, described driving a bomb-laden bus as, "just like driving a really big Pinto.") Twenty-seven deaths in Pinto collision fires and subsequent product liability suits are what happened.

> Critics argued that the vehicles' lack of a true rear bumper as well as any reinforcing structure between the rear panel and the tank, meant that in certain conditions, the tank would be thrust forward into the differential, which had a number of protruding bolts that could puncture the tank. This, and the fact that doors could potentially jam during an accident (due to poor reinforcing) made the car a potential deathtrap ("Ford Pinto," 2006).

By the time the 1991 *Grimshaw v. Ford Motor Company* product liability case was litigated, *Forbes Magazine* had included the Pinto on its list of the ten worst cars of all time. In the years following there appeared law review papers arguing that the case against Ford was less clear-cut than first believed ("Ford Pinto," 2006). Unfortunately for Ford, these papers have received very little attention outside of law school classes, leaving the Pinto with an infamous place in automobile history.

The well-publicized Pinto collision explosions combined with the movie "Class Action" educated the American public in the practice of *cost-benefit analysis*. In a cost-benefit analysis the expense of an automobile's feature is weighed against the profit or loss it would produce. For example, the expense of adding reinforcement to a car's doors to make it a safer vehicle might increase the sticker price enough to reduce sales. Another type of cost-benefit analysis has sinister implications. It is the calculation of the expense of a recall for a safety concern compared to the cost of anticipated litigation and lawsuit settlements. It was never established that Ford knew the Pinto was prone to collision explosions and decided to let the accidents happen rather than have a recall. However, the media and urban myth combined to give the impression that Ford did make that calculation. Although a misperception, it raises the ethical question, "Would it have been morally wrong if Ford knew about the Pinto's problem but decided against a recall as a result of a cost-benefit analysis?"

This case also raises a value theory question. If Ford actually calculated a cost-benefit analysis it implies the company's willingness to weigh consumer safety against the expense of a recall. The philosopher Immanuel Kant believed that because nothing is more valuable than human beings, decisions should reflect what is best for them. He would argue that where human life is concerned a cost-benefit analysis is unnecessary. For Kant, if a recall would save even a single life it should occur. The argument against Kant's position is that the executives at Ford had a responsibility to the stockholders to maximize profit. Caring for humanity is not part of the executives' job description. Kant is free to put people first in his own affairs, but he has no authority to impose his moral standard on others. Whenever a cost-benefit analysis occurs, the monetary benefit of one action is being weighed against another. This does not mean that a cost-benefit analysis will be the determining factor. Other considerations might come into play. In the Pinto case, Kant's argument or the risk of a public relations disaster could have resulted in a recall.

Chapter Five

Aesthetics

A classic—something that everybody wants to have read and nobody wants to read.

—Mark Twain

In the movie "Dead Poets Society" an English teacher, portrayed by Robin Williams, expresses his disagreement with the author of the literature textbook by insisting that the students rip out the book's introductory pages. In the book's introduction the author provides a formula for evaluating the greatness of a poem. Williams' character, Mr. Keating, explains to his students that the greatness of a literary piece cannot be calculated and numerically expressed. He argues that poetry appeals to our emotions, and since an emotional response to a poem cannot be calibrated, the greatness of a poem cannot be quantified.

People's opinions of books, movies, music, and paintings vary. Even critics give mixed reviews of artistic works. Disagreement among experts as well as non-experts implies that beauty is, indeed, in the eyes of the beholder. Consider that Oprah Winfrey, Jim Carrey, Harrison Ford, Jennifer Lopez, and Hallie Barry all have been featured in *People Magazine's* annual "50 Most Beautiful People" issue. Such diversity raises the question: "What makes a person beautiful?" Sensation is what we see, hear, taste, feel, and smell. Perception is the interpretation of what the senses have provided. Ten people might look at the actress Angelie Jolie and five consider her stunningly beautiful; three evaluate her as somewhat attractive; and two describe her as rather ordinary. *Aesthetics* is the subcategory of philosophy devoted to the study of those things that are pleasing to the senses. It is concerned with questions like: *What makes something beautiful to see or pleasant to hear? What are the qualities that make a literary or musical work a classic?*

The word aesthetic is derived from the Greek word *aesthetes* which means, "a person who perceives." Note that *aesthetes* refers to perception and not sensation. Sensation is the experience of seeing, hearing, smelling, tasting or feeling. Perception is the meaning we assign to the information our senses have provided. Sensation is a physical experience; perception is intellectual and emotional. An art connoisseur and a four-year-old would see the same images and colors looking at a Van Gogh painting and have different thoughts and feelings while looking. This example raises the question of the nature of beauty. Is beauty "out there" in the object or "in here" within the observer?

Aesthetics is related to *value theory*, the topic of the previous chapter. It is remarkable that a Van Gogh painting ("Sunflowers") that did not have a single buyer during the artist's lifetime was sold at auction for 39.9 million dollars in 1987. What change of conditions account for a painting going from worthless to virtually priceless? Art collectors in Van Gogh's day saw the same images and colors on canvas seen by contemporary art collectors. Yet, the perceptions of the two groups are very different. Whatever the explanation for this difference, it involves both aesthetics and value theory.

Aesthetic questions can be asked about changes in style. Perhaps you have seen a photograph of your parents from the 1960's and were amused by their Afro hairstyle, bell-bottom pants, and tie-dyed shirts. (They themselves might even cringe at the sight of what they once considered *cool*.) Also, there was a time when a shaved head was the result of losing a bet or taking a dare and only sailors and convicts adorned themselves with tattoos. Whether it is a Van Gogh painting or a work of body art, the question is, *What are the conditions that influence our perception of beauty and experience of sensual pleasure?*

One way of approaching this question is to consider what makes a classic a classic. The highest praise a critic can give a book or movie is that it is "destined to be a classic." But what does this mean? Mark Twain's wry observation that a classic is, "something that everybody wants to have read and nobody wants to read" is witty but not helpful (Negri, p. 36). A more useful description of a classic is that it is a work that establishes or measures up to a standard of excellence by meeting at least one of three qualifications:

(1) It has passed the test of time by maintaining popularity or recognition over several generations. This is the characteristic of *endurance*.
(2) It has appeal to a diversity of cultures. This is the characteristic of *universality*.
(3) It has the good opinion of recognized experts. As stated previously, experts will disagree. However, a consensus of authorities must recog-

nize it as a classic if it is to be a classic. This is the characteristic of *recognition*.

An interesting situation occurs when experts are overruled by public acclaim. The books of Stephen King have been panned by literary critics and King himself has described his writing as, "the literary equivalent of a Big Mac and fries" (*60 Minutes*). Similarly, Robert James Waller's *The Bridges of Madison County* received numerous unfavorable reviews in spite of its 150 week run on the *New York Times* bestseller list and distinction of being the all-time best-selling hardcover fiction book, having surpassed *Gone with the Wind*. Lucy Maude Montgomery received numerous rejections before the publication of her classic, *Anne of Green Gables*. The musical "Les Miserables" met with unfavorable reviews when it debuted in 1980. Yet, it went on to a twenty-five year run and achieve international and Tony award recognition. Aesthetics is the philosopher's attempt to explain why certain things appeal to our sense of beauty and experience of pleasure.

Chapter Six

Metaphysics

What a piece of work is a man! how noble in reason! how infinite in faculty! in form and moving how express and admirable! in action how like an angel! in apprehension how like a god! And yet, what is this quintessence of dust?

Hamlet, Act II, Scene 2

I see dead people.

—Cole Sear, "The Sixth Sense"

Consider several goldfish swimming around in a fishbowl. What is *reality* to them? Spatially, the extent of their existence is the fishbowl. Temporally, the extent of their existence is however many days, weeks, months or years they will live. Their reality does not extend beyond their life span within the fishbowl. Of course, there is a world beyond the fishbowl. The fishbowl is in a room; which is in a house; which is in a neighborhood; which is in a city; which is in a country; etc. Outside of the fishbowl there are people and other organisms carrying on innumerable activities; most of which have no direct effect on the goldfish. Further, there was a time when neither the bowl nor the fish existed and there will come a time when, again, neither will exist—at least, not in the present form. Assuming that goldfish do not think, they are not curious about the possibility of any *reality* outside of their bowl.

Human beings do think and some of us are curious about the dimensions of our reality. Like the goldfish, we have a spatial reality. How far does this reality extend for us? The universe is the totality of matter—the cosmos. Is there reality outside of the universe? Are there entities that are not physical and, therefore, cannot be detected by the senses? Like the goldfish, we have a temporal reality. The concepts of past, present, and future are meaningful to us and we experience the passing of time in precise units of seconds, minutes, hours, years, decades, etc. When did time begin and will it ever end? Perhaps we are like characters in a book for whom "time" began on page one and ends on the last page. Is there a sequence of events outside of our "book" that only resembles what we refer to as time?

The word *abstruse* means, "hard to understand; profound" (*Webster's*, 1984, p. 6). The word *abstract* means, "having no material existence; theoretical rather than practical" (*Webster's*, 1984, p. 6). There is no branch of philosophy more abstruse and abstract than *metaphysics*. Metaphysics is the study of reality and is derived from the combination of the Greek words for "after" (*meta*) and "physics" (*phusika*). In the early collections of Aristotle's works, metaphysics came after his writings on physics. Science investigates and describes the physical world by observation and experimentation. Science is concerned with material reality. Metaphysics is concerned with *ultimate* or *final* reality. Theoretically, after science has answered all questions pertaining to physical reality and metaphysics has answered all questions pertaining to nonphysical reality then reality will have been studied ultimately. It will be a metaphysician who will declare, "There is nothing left to study."

The scientist acquires information by way of observation and experimentation. The metaphysician uses reason alone to provide answers. (A question like, *"Why does the universe exist?"* cannot be answered scientifically.) The fundamental question of metaphysics is: *Can ultimate reality be grasped by the five senses, or is ultimate reality supernatural and outside of space and time?* To return to the goldfish in the fishbowl; if they could engage in metaphysics they would ask, "Is there anything outside of this fishbowl?" and "How did this fishbowl come into existence or has it always existed?" (And, yes, they would be curious about their food source; the changing of their water; and what became of those fish that disappeared after floating on the surface.)

Not being goldfish, we have different—but similar—questions about the dimensions of our reality. Our metaphysical questions include:

- Is the universe eternal or did it come into existence by way of a prior entity? (Was the universe created? If so, who or what created it and for what purpose, if any?)—Is there an afterlife existence for human beings? (What will happen to us when we die?)
- Is there a nonphysical dimension of reality? (Currently, we inhabit a material world contained in space and time. Is there a so-called spiritual realm that cannot be detected by the senses?)
- Does God exist as an entity outside of space and time in a dimension referred to as eternity?

- Is there something more to human beings than our physical attributes? (Exactly what do we mean when we use terms like *spirit* and *mind*?)

Most people do not regularly wrestle with these questions. Nevertheless, these questions have significance in certain situations. A school board deliberating on whether or not to include the theory of *intelligent design* in the science curriculum has to consider the question of the origin of the universe. People in bereavement over the loss of a loved one and terminal patients facing their imminent death contemplate the afterlife question. Parents considering church attendance as a family will consider the existence of God and the value of a spiritual life. The questions of choice-making and responsibility are relevant in interpersonal relationships as well as criminal trials. If we are to be held responsible for our behavior there must be an understanding of the terms *human being* and *free will*.

Instead of addressing numerous metaphysical questions, to help you understand metaphysics, two issues will be addressed in the remainder of this chapter: (1) The Mind-Body Problem and (2) The Existence of God.

THE MIND-BODY PROBLEM

Remember the words *abstruse* and *abstract*? The "Mind-Body Problem" is a philosophical issue that is especially difficult to understand and highly conceptual. The "Mind-Body Problem" is the problem of explaining the relationship, supposing there is one, between the mind and the body, supposing that the mind is immaterial and the body is material. Another way of framing this issue is to ask: *Is there a nonphysical dimension to human beings?* That is, perhaps we have a *spiritual* component—a part of us that is not physical but nonetheless real.

If we do not have a nonphysical component then we are merely highly evolved organisms driven by biology and influenced by conditioning, like Pavlov's dog. If this is true, then *free will* and *responsibility* are illusions, that is, they are misperceptions of reality. However, if free will actually exists then we have control of our thoughts and actions, making us responsible for them. If there is a nonphysical reality to human beings then what is it? Further, since it is not biological in its origin, what is its source? Further still, why does it exist? *What is the benefit of the nonphysical entity referred to as the conscience? Why should anyone be concerned with the meaning of life since it is merely a concept and unnecessary for survival?*

Rene Descartes, the seventeenth French philosopher and mathematician, gave considerable attention to the "Mind-Body Problem." A *dualist*,

Descartes believed that reality consists of two fundamentally different entities. It is not difficult to understand dualism if we go no further than saying that all of reality is composed of physical and nonphysical entities. The challenge of the "Mind-Body Problem" is to describe the bridge between the material (matter) and nonmaterial (mind) components. Posed as a question: *How can something that is nonphysical have an effect on something that is physical?* Through the centuries, both before and after Descartes, many philosophers have attempted to explain this causal connection, but none have succeeded in solving this mystery in such a way that it is a settled issue.

The existence of a mind-body connection is accepted in medicine. Peptic (stomach) ulcers can be induced by emotional stress. This condition is referred to as *psychosomatic*, a term combining the Greek words for soul (*psuche*) and body (*soma*). Biofeedback is a treatment for hypertension (and other disorders) in which patients lower their blood pressure by engaging in self-talk or meditation that relaxes them. In biofeedback electronic instruments monitor the patients' progress, spurring them on to more success. The placebo effect is an established phenomenon in research that tests the effectiveness of medications. In sports, athletes speak of "psyching-up" as part of preparing for competition. World records are rarely broken in practice; the mental state of athletes in competition contributes to their best performance. It is not an overstatement to say that the influence of the mind upon the body is an assumption of science. The "Mind-Body Problem" seeks to explain how the nonphysical comes into contact with and affects the physical.

One solution to this problem is theological, positing that it is by supernatural means that the immaterial connects with and influences the material. How could there be a natural explanation for the mind's influence on the body since the mind is not part of the natural (or material) world? The solution to the "Mind-Body Problem" is to be found, at least in part, in the realm of the supernatural. This solution implies the existence of God as the means by which the supernatural intersects with the natural order. This brings us to the second issue: *the existence of God*.

THE EXISTENCE OF GOD

A thorough consideration of what is implied by the use of the word *god* would require a separate book. For our purposes, the dictionary definition is adequate: "In monotheistic religions, the creator and ruler of the universe, regarded as eternal, infinite, all-powerful, and all-knowing; Supreme Being; Almighty" (*Webster's*, 1984, p. 599).

"I believe in God" is a faith statement. Disbelief in God's existence (atheism) is a faith position as well. In chapter one (Epistemology) scientific, historical, and philosophical truth are described along with their respective methods for investigating truth claims. Since there is no experiment that could demonstrate God's existence it is not possible to prove scientifically that God exists. While there are innumerable people, both living and dead, who have expressed their belief in God, these testimonies do not constitute historical proof of God's existence. Although God's existence cannot be proven by the application of logic, many philosophers have offered arguments for the existence of God. Although these philosophical arguments are often referred to as the *rational proofs for God's existence*, they are actually attempts by philosophers to make a case for belief in God. As you read the following descriptions of these arguments, you will recognize that they do not prove God's existence beyond a reasonable doubt. Instead, they provide reasons why belief in God is rational. When taken together, they make belief in God reasonable.

THE ONTOLOGICAL ARGUMENT

This argument is associated with Saint Anselm, an eleventh century Christian philosopher, who put forth the idea that human beings have an idea of a perfect being. Anselm went on to state that since actual existence is better than imaginary existence the perfect being must have the better quality — actual existence. There is no shortage of philosophers who have evaluated this argument and concluded that it is weak. Their response is that there is no proof that all human beings have an idea of a perfect being and, even if they did, it is possible to imagine things that do not actually exist.

THE COSMOLOGICAL ARGUMENT

"Nothing is the cause of itself" is a logical statement since in order for something to be its own cause it would have to exist and not exist at the same time. The cosmological argument applies this causation principle to the universe. Since the universe could not be its own cause it follows that it must have a creator. In this argument God is the "universe maker." The counter to this argument is that the causation principle applies to God as well. This raises the question: *Who or what created God?* If this question is answered, "God has no creator — God has always existed," a skeptic would then ask, "If an eternal God is a possibility then why not an eternal universe?"

TELEOLOGICAL ARGUMENT

The eighteenth century British philosopher William Paley presented one of the best-known metaphors in the history of philosophy with his *watchmaker analogy*. He reasoned that anyone encountering a watch would admit that there must be watchmaker. A watch is an instrument that is too complicated in its structure and too precise in its operation to consider it the product of random events. The teleological argument states that the universe's order, harmony, and predictability imply an intelligent being responsible for its existence. This intelligent being is God.

Giving respectability to this argument are these words from Albert Einstein, the renown physicist who did not believe in a personal God: "I believe in Spinoza's God who reveals himself in the orderly harmony of what exists, not in a God who concerns himself with fates and actions of human beings" (Dukas and Hoffman, 1981, p. 32).

MORAL ARGUMENT

This argument was used in the eighteenth century by the German philosopher Immanuel Kant and in the twentieth century by C.S. Lewis, a defender of the Christian faith. Both men argued that the desire for justice implies God's existence as Lawgiver and Judge. Kant believed that without God there would be no way for one individual or culture to disapprove of another. Lewis agreed, saying that the concept of justice would be meaningless unless God exists as the One Who requires certain behaviors of all human beings and eventually will administer justice to all.

THE ETHNOLOGICAL ARGUMENT

Ethnology is the study of *cultural organizations*, also referred to as *institutions*. Among all of the peoples and tribes of the earth there are religious institutions. Of course, the religions of humankind are numerous and diverse. Nevertheless, it is significant that wherever and whenever people have lived, they have engaged in some form of worship. The ethnological argument is that it is in the nature of human beings to have an interest in the supernatural and a curiosity about a Supreme Being. The explanation for this is that God has made human beings in this way so that they will seek relationship with the divine. Saint Augustine expressed this concept with the words: "You have made us for yourself, O Lord, and our hearts are restless until they rest in You" (397 A.D.).

Conclusion

As stated in the title, this book was written for students taking a philosophy course who are either indifferent to the subject or struggling to understand it. This book is a *primer*—a textbook that explains the basic principles of philosophy. No primer, however well-written, can substitute for reading, contemplating, and discussing the ideas generated by centuries of renown philosophers. If this little book has been helpful to you in your study of philosophy then it has served its purpose. If it has demystified the subject and encouraged you to think more philosophically, then this book has gone beyond its intention. Thirty-five years ago Thomas Ellis Katen, author of one of the finest books written for philosophy students, wrote:

> The study of philosophy can lead us to new discoveries and insights about ourselves and the world. If we really get into philosophy, it will get into us, for there is great power in ideas—power that can move men and nations and even worlds. There is also great pleasure in struggling with and gaining mastery over such ideas (1973, p. xiii).

I agree with Professor Katen and this is why I teach philosophy.

Glossary

Absolute Truth (Absolutism): A belief that is unaffected by circumstances is a belief that is held *absolutely*. To believe something *absolutely* is to believe it unconditionally; that there are no circumstances that will alter the belief.

Abstract: The characteristic of being conceptual rather than physical.

Abstruse: The characteristic of being profound and difficult to understand.

Aesthetics: It is the subcategory of philosophy concerned with understanding the experience of beauty and pleasure. It addresses the question of why certain things are pleasing to the senses.

Anecdotal Data: Information resulting from experiences rather than formal research. Such information can be a single case or collection of several cases.

Argument: A presentation that supports a point-of-view; a case for accepting something as true.

Argumentum ad Baculum: (Argument of Force) A logical fallacy in which fear or intimidation is used to support an idea.

Argumentum ad Ignorantium: (Argument of Ignorance) A logical fallacy in which an absence of proof of something is erroneously concluded as proof of its absence.

Argumentum ad Vercundiam: (Argument of Authority) A logical fallacy in which an expert in one field provides an opinion that is irrelevant because the topic under consideration is outside of the expert's field.

Aristotle's Principle of the Golden Mean: Aristotle characterized a virtue as the apex (i.e. high-point) between two vices. For example, courage is the virtue located between the two vices of recklessness and cowardice.

Cause-and-Effect: A relationship in which event-A precedes event-B and it can be demonstrated that event-A is the reason why event-B occurred.

Cogito ergo sum: ("I think, therefore, I am.") One of philosophy's best-known quotations, these are the words of Rene Descartes. He concluded that his existence was the one thing of which he could be certain. Even if every other thought he had was incorrect, the fact that he was thinking proved his existence.

Correlation: A relationship between two events tending to occur together, calling for further investigation of the relationship.

Cost-Benefit Analysis: The practice in business and industry of comparing the expense of two or more courses of action to help decide which one to take.

Cosmological Argument: One of the so-called *rational proofs for the existence of God* by which it is reasoned that the universe could not have created itself. In this argument God is referred to as the *universe-maker*.

Deductive Reasoning: The logical process by which a conclusion necessarily follows from principles; thinking from general to specific. For example, it might be concluded that Abraham Lincoln was a great President if criteria for "presidential greatness" (general) are established and Lincoln (specific) meets the criteria.

Deontological Ethics: The determination of moral behavior based upon a duty to obey certain rules of conduct. The Ten Commandments is an example of a deontological code of conduct. The term deontological is derived from the Greek word for "duty" (*deon*).

Dualism: The belief that reality consists of two fundamentally different entities: the physical and the nonphysical. Dualism is related to the *mind-body problem*.

Empirical: The characteristic of demonstration to show that something is true. Scientific experiments are commonly referred to as empirical proof.

Endurance: In aesthetic philosophy, this is one of the three criteria by which a work of art, literature or music is evaluated as a classic. *Endurance* refers to a work having passed the test of time. The other two criteria are *universality* and *recognition*.

Epistemology: The subcategory of philosophy concerned with knowledge. Specifically, it is concerned with how knowledge is acquired and the means by which certainty of knowledge is achieved.

Ethics: The subcategory of philosophy concerned with right moral conduct.

Ethnological Argument: One of the so-called *rational proofs for the existence of God*, it is based on the belief that all races and cultures of human beings throughout history have practiced religion. This curiosity about the supernatural and a Supreme Being is the result of God having made people in such a way as to investigate a religious life.

Fallacy: This is the general term for any error in logic; a flaw in reasoning.

Fallacy of Causal Connection: A logical fallacy in which one event or condition is erroneously believed to be the explanation for another event or condition. This implies that the correct explanation has been overlooked.

Free Will: In philosophy, this is understood as the ability to make authentic choices; to act in accordance with one's strongest motive. It is widely believed that free will makes human beings responsible for their behavior.

God: In monotheistic (one-god) religions, God is the Supreme Being with the qualities of omniscience (all-knowing), omnipotence (all-powerful), ubiquitous (present everywhere), and pre-existence (prior to the universe).

Happiness: In both philosophy and psychology this is understood as overall contentment with one's life.

Historical Proof: One of the three categories of truth, it is knowledge of the past based on testimony.

Intervening Variable: Related to the fallacy of causal connection, it is the overlooked event or condition that is the correct explanation for the event or condition under investigation. For example, the correct explanation for the high rate of suicide among police officers is not the nature of their work but the immediate availability of a firearm.

Inductive Reasoning: This is a logical process that progresses from specific to general. For example, the criteria for "great Presidents" would be *deduced* from first making a list of great Presidents and then evaluating what they had in common.

Law of Non-Contradiction: This is the rule of logic that a statement cannot be true if it speaks against itself. For example, the statement, "There is no truth" negates itself, because if *there is no truth* it would include the statement itself.

Logic: The subcategory of philosophy that is concerned with correct reasoning.

Metaphysics: The subcategory of philosophy that is concerned with reality outside of the physical realm; it addresses questions that cannot be investigated scientifically or historically. Examples of metaphysical questions are: *How did the universe come into existence? Does God exist? Is there an afterlife? What is the meaning of life?*

Mind-Body Problem: If human beings have a nonphysical entity that directs the mental processes (i.e. the mind), how does that which is nonphysical contact and influence that which is physical (i.e. the body)?

Moral Argument: One of the so-called *rational proofs for the existence of God* by which it is reasoned that if justice is to have any meaning there must be an ultimate Judge (God). Injustice often prevails in the world. Nevertheless, the longing for justice is so great that it must be more than a mere concept, implying a judge (God) who is able to administer justice outside of human history.

Ontological Argument: Perhaps the weakest of the *so-called rational proofs for the existence of God* in which God is defined as the greatest Being imaginable. As such, God has all good qualities to the infinite degree. Since actual existence is better than imaginary existence, God must have actual existence. Therefore, God exists.

Ought: This is a one-word summary of ethical philosophy, referring to how people *should* behave.

Overgeneralization: The logical fallacy of saying too much from too little data. A common instance of this fallacy is assuming a principle from a single case or event.

Philosophical Proof: The test for truth used by philosophers in contrast to the methods employed by historians and scientists. Historical truth is established by way of evidence and testimony. Scientific truth is demonstrated by experimentation. A philosopher tests a statement for truth by asking three questions: (1) Does this statement contradict itself? (2) Does this statement correspond to reality as demonstrated by science and experienced by most people? (3) Is this statement of practical use? Although a philosopher's methodology cannot always verify a statement, it can often falsify a statement.

Philosophy: Defined as the love and pursuit of wisdom by intellectual means; *philosophy* is derived from the Greek words for love (*philein*) and knowledge (*sophos*).

Plato's Allegory of the Cave: This is Plato's representation of human beings as chained in place by their culture, education, and experience and therefore unable to attain complete knowledge. Plato believed that individuals, at best, can have a perspective on the truth of a subject.

Plato's Concept of the Mind: Plato conceptualized the mind (the entity that directs the mental processes) as consisting of *appetites* (feelings), *reason* (intellect), and the *spirited element* (the person each of us would like to be). He reasoned that when feelings and intellect were in conflict, the spirited element could influence the person to act honorably.

Primer: A textbook that explains the basic principles of a subject.

Psychology: The science of mind and behavior that attempts to explain why people think, act, and feel as they do. An alternative definition is *the study of human behavior*.

Plausible Rival Hypothesis: An alternative explanation that is compatible with the facts of an event and therefore acceptable.

Rational Proofs for God's Existence: The five arguments that favor the existence of God: *cosmological, ethnological, moral, ontological,* and *teleological*. Although referred to as "proofs," they are attempts to make an intellectual case for the existence of God.

Recognition: A term used in aesthetic philosophy that refers to experts' opinion that a work of art is a classic. *Endurance* and *universality* are two other criteria used in evaluating a work as a classic.

Relative Truth (Relativism): In contrast to *absolutism*, relativism refers to something that is true under certain conditions. For example, when someone speaks of something as absolutely true it means that there are no conditions that will make it untrue. If something is relatively true it means that it is true only under certain conditions.

Religion: Although frequently defined as a system of worship expressing belief in a god or gods, an alternative definition is *intensive and comprehensive belief*.

Scientific Proof: The methodology for establishing something as true by way of the four-step procedure of observation, hypothesis, experimentation, and conclusion. This type of proof is also referred to as *empirical demonstration*.

Skeptic: One who habitually doubts; historically, a follower of the Greek philosopher Pyrrho of Elis.

Syllogism: A form of deductive reasoning used in logic and consisting of a major premise, minor premise, and conclusion. A common illustration of a syllogism is: All men are mortal (major premise) . . . Socrates is a man (minor premise) . . . Therefore, Socrates is mortal (conclusion).

Teleological Argument: One of the five so-called *rational proofs for the existence of God* in which it is stated that order and predictability in the universe imply that the universe is not the product of random events but an intelligent design. The *intelligent designer* is God.

Teleological Ethics: In contrast to *deontological ethics*, teleological ethical systems determine moral right by the achievement of a desired goal. Teleological is derived from the Greek word for "end" (*telos*). Teleological ethics can be characterized by the phrase "the end justifies the means."

Universality: A term from aesthetic philosophy and one of the three criteria for evaluating a work of art as a classic. If an artistic work has appeal among a diversity of cultures then it is said to have universality. *Endurance* and *recognition* are the other two criteria.

Value Theory: The subcategory of philosophy concerned with the evaluation of the worth of something. It is often applied in decision-making when the relative worth of two things are part of a decision-making process.

References

INTRODUCTION

Aristotle. *Nichomachean ethics*. Book I, Chapter 6. translated: James Weldon. 1897. New York: MacMillan.

Frankl, V. 1946. *Man's search for meaning*. New York: Washington Square Press.

Freud, S. 1935. *A general introduction to psychoanalysis*. New York: Washington Square Press.

Heidegger, M. 1956. "The Way back into the Ground of Metaphysics."in *Existentialsim from Dostoevski to Sartre*. Ed. Walter Kaufmann. New York: Meridian Books.

James, W. 1994. *Varieties of Religious Experience*. New York: Modern Library.

——. 1995. "The Current Dilemma of Philosophy." *Pragmatism*. Mineola, New York: Dover Publications.

Johnson, T.L. 2007."Practical Philosophy: The Greco-Roman Moralists." Chantilly, VA: The Teaching Company.

Jung, C.G. 1933. *Modern man in search of a soul*. New York: Harcourt Brace Jovanovich Publishers.

Kohn, A. 2004. *What does it mean to be educated?* Boston: Beacon Press.

Myers, D. 1992. *The pursuit of happiness: Who is happy and why*. New York: William Morrow and Company.

Plato. *Apology*. 38A. translated: Hugh tredennick. 1961. *The collected dialogues*. ed. Edith Hamilton and Huntington Carnes. New York: Pantheon Books.

Perry, J. and Bratman, M. 1998. *Introduction to philosophy: classical and contemporary readings*. New York: Oxford University Press.

Popkin, R. and Stroll, A. 1993. *Philosophy made easy*. New York: Bantam Doubleday Publishing Group, Inc.

Price, S. 2004. *1001 smartest things ever said*. Guilford, CT: The Lyons Press.

Russell, B. 1910. *The problem of philosophy*. Oxford, England: Oxford University Press.

Yalom, I. 1989. *Love's executioner*. New York: Basic Books, Inc.

CHAPTER ONE

New York Times. July 3, 1990.
Szasz, T. 1973. *The second sin.* Garden City, New York: Anchor Press Doubleday.
Price, S. 2004. *1001 Smartest Things Ever Said.* Guilford, CT: The Lyons Press.

CHAPTER TWO

Price, S. 2004. *1001 dumbest things ever said.* Guilford, CT: The Lyons press.
Shakespeare, W. circa 1602. *Hamlet.* 3.1.
Shneidman, E. 1996. *The suicidal mind.* New York: Oxford University Press.
Spence, G. 1996. *How to argue and win every time.* New York: St. Martin's Press.

CHAPTER THREE

Aristotle. *Nichomachean ethics.* Book I, Chapter 6. translated: James Weldon. 1897. New York: MacMillan.
Martin, M. 1995. *Everyday morality: an introduction to applied ethics.* Belmont, CA: Wadsworth Publishing Company.
Pope, A. (circa) 1744. *An Essay on Man.* Epistle 1. New York: Prentice Hall.
Szasz, T. 1973. *The second sin.* New York: Doubleday.
Tennyson, A. 1870. "The Charge of the Light Brigade." Boston, MA: J.E. Tilton and Company.

CHAPTER FOUR

"Ford Pinto," Wikepedia. Recovered from http://en.wikipedia.org on July 20, 2006.
Peck, S. 1985. *The people of the lie: the hope for healing human evil.* New York: Touchstone Books.

CHAPTER FIVE

Negri, P. (General Editor). 1999. *The wit and wisdom of Mark Twain.* Mineola, NY: Dover Publications, Inc.
Sixty Minutes: Leslie Stahl's Interview with Stephen King. New York: ABC.

CHAPTER SIX

Augustine. 397 A.D. *The Confessions of Saint Augustine*. Translated by J. Warner. 1963. New York: Penguin Books.

Dukas, H. and Hoffman, B. (Editors). 1981. *The human side*. Princeton, NJ: Princeton University Press.

Webster's New World Dictionary. 1984. New York: Random House.

CONCLUSION

Katen, T.E. 1973. *Doing philosophy*. Englewood Cliffs, NJ. Prentice Hall Publishing.